SHADOW WORK

Tavius Dyer

Palamedes

San Francisco

Palamedes Publishing
www.palamedes.pub
San Francisco

Cover by Kate Marchio
www.katemarchiophotography.com

Cover photography by Monica Renee Martin
www.monicamartin.org

ISBN 978-0-9996930-7-0
LCCN 2018933078

Also available in ebook:
Kindle b4873897-e2cf-4bf5-a7d1-dd8acb8f0c8c
EPUB 55cdf9e3-7c0a-4219-b539-8e95c9e361ec
www.palamedes.pub/books/shadow-work

www.facebook.com/PalamedesPub
www.twitter.com/PalamedesPub
www.instagram.com/PalamedesPub

I dedicate this book to all who struggle with recovery from addiction, grief, trauma, and mental illness. I dedicate this book to my beautiful boy Gabriel. He taught me love and kindness, calling me "Daddy" even into his teens. He gave the most affectionate hugs too. He also gave me the inspiration and motivation to learn, grow, and change my life for the better. My son is the main reason I am alive today. He has blessed me with many things, including the opportunity to help myself and take care of myself, the greatest gifts. I love you son! You continue to teach me and make me proud by the life you chose to live and all the people you loved. You made such a difference in our lives with your love.

Shadow Work

I

We cast a shadow
Of doubt
Within

When we hold on to
What we don't like

About ourselves

What we hide

From the light
Within

Afraid of exposure

Afraid of
Letting others see

All of ourselves

For fear of rejection
Not being good enough

Not being worthy
Of others

And their love

But within the darkness
Is opportunity for light

To search out the dark corners of our minds and hearts

To expose the reality
Of our fears

And the reality
Our fears

Made

Instead

Of the lives
Our hearts

Ache for
But cannot

Reach
Or grasp

Because the things we hold on to

Become us

And do not allow us

To grasp
Something new

So fear not
The light

II

Let the shadow go

And expose the truth
You hide
Within

To yourself
And let the world in

It will be okay

You do not need anyone else

But

All of yourself

Must Everything

I sip cold coffee
Try to remember

My first kiss
Or the cul-de-sac

Drive-through childhood
I did not order

And since super-sizing
My mind

Never made me Jesus

The sky has become a puzzle

I have not yet picked up the pieces
And put them back together

Instead

I am afraid of
Affirmation

And art
Has become

The act of learning
To love myself

Nothing but
The exploration

Of everything
Until I settle

On something

Rock Bottom Renaissance

Stoned stupid smart on

Purple Cush
Prozac and two dollar pints

I snaked through crowds
So proud of themselves

Smiles forced face lifts and tucks
As if age couldn't get the better of them

But my bungee cord belt
Buck ninety-nine baby blue flops

Neon tee and pant shorts
Hung off my junk did

Exposing

Bright light green soccer shorts
Tight to my tush till

I turned my insides out
Too many times

To bloody stool
And beer glass in fist

Upside the bouncer's heavy head
To the floor

Cop car
Steel cuffs

And a concrete room with a metal bunk

Only to ponder Hegelian History
As Brahms' second symphony

Brings past to present

Shaped
As a river flows

Karaoke Killer

Been called that
When

Nothing frightened me more
Than what I wanted

Chased pills with precious poison

Puffed blueberry bud
Till purple haze became a mic in my mouth

Shoutin' out
I got

Bopped in the head
Wrestled to the ground

Between

The booze and blood
I chucked from the bottom of my gut

Eighty-sixed as quick as a hot dish

And when they had no reason
I gave them one

Threw a speaker across the karaoke stage
While someone sung

And took off running

Down the train tracks
In my flip flops

Until found hours later
Alone at a table

At an all night diner
In a black out

Telephone Holiday

This year's roast beef will be pre-cooked

My brothers and sisters
Still believe in Santa

My mother pours out
And all I can do to love

Is listen

The real problem
Is my being

Locked up

And she asks me

What's this all about
As our silence gives way to line noise

Hundreds of miles away
And I smell her banquet

Every detail fills my senses

Puts me
There

Reminds me
What life

Was like

Once upon a time

White Minority

He's a little man
Snores like a dragon

Carries the keys to the homies' car

We attempt everything

Before someone else throws
An empty cardboard lunch box

To wake him up

And he sees me

A privileged minority
Among minorities

A gringo in jail

I am
What represents

Their oppression

A white guy

And educated
Made worse

Home boy
Flies over

And looks down at me
As I lay on my rack

Another
Gets up and approaches

From behind me

Yet another

Springs off his rack
From the side

These inmates
All want a piece of me

But I already have two strikes
And I am not going to

Strike out in jail

So I learn to laugh
At their threats

Welcome the punishment
Take all of their power

By not reacting

Instead
Egging them on

Welcome the beating
Hysterically

Luckily
Especially incarcerated

Crazy trumps all

Love Made Me

With rain comes
The season of my release

Yesterday grew wings
Wind cannot resist

A behavior that took
The world away

Turned me into
My own

Spiraling descent
Chaotic

If not for destination

Constant arrival

These weeks
Go by

Like days
Outside

And it all
Begins to blur

As if blinded

By the tears I had
But couldn't show

Pen Point

Mind pointed as pen to the page
Why such a pointed thing

Everything
One
Time is space's
Relativity

Projections
Reflected

In the womb
Of this world

Rumi might tell tales

Be melting snow
Wean yourself of yourself

Until the thirsty fish
Inside of you

Has enough of what it's thirsty for

He must be hallucinating
Or drunk on spirits

I'm drunk on dreams
My days are dreams

So many pages
In a picture book

Not my own

A story
I cannot hear

Until written

Creative Expression Is Self-Exploration

To write is to pour forth
Pen to page

Or fingers
Caterpillar-like
On keys

Perhaps
Running the stem of a rose bud

Only to cocoon
And birth

The beauty of a butterfly

We witness this
A transformation of the senses

Imagination plus a fire
That burns between the lines

Words unseen

An utterance
A sound
A sight

All of these things compile
Themselves within us

Take new form
One person to the next

Coloring

THIS moment

Which is

ALL

That truly
Exists

Here

Now

At a Café

Conversations
Crinkle

Rise

As the exhaust of what we say

Writing
These words

Become paper
Crumpled

Fingers into fists

Tossed

In the waste basket

In the corner of my mind

An unquenchable thirst
For formlessness

Despite
The sight and sound

These words become
In your mind

Adult Children

Not authorized
To have feelings

We took the stage
In the presence of others

To act out
The stories

We told ourselves

Allowing

The dreams we dreamt
But hadn't lived

Become our memories

We stayed up weeks
Manufacturing

The fear
Of coming down

A continuum of uncontrollable acts
Orbited our every move

As our specific gravity
Held moons captive

The hostages
We took

Where merely
Ourselves

Chasing one peak
Experience

After another

Until long after
The experience

Faded

Burnt out

Like unseen stars
Falling to earth at night

Above the canopy of light
In the busy city

Below

Separation

To be separated

But not
Separate

How is this so

Relationships can be this way

The married couple
Now roommates

Pretend to be friends
And then that ends

However
Remain under one roof

No longer
Sharing the same bed

Distance can be painful
Especially when so close

Like the slow pull of a band aid
Tearing each hair

One by one

Instead of a quick tug

And one final

Sensation

Anyone's Neighbor

A swirl of caffeine crystals
At the bottom

Of my dried out
Coffee cup

Looks like still brown waves
Upon an empty sea

Or the end of a batch of Meth
Cooked atop the stove at home

Often our only meal
For sleepless winter weeks

Steamed off glass
Pyrex pie plates

Crackback scraped
Fluffs to snow

Like frost on ice cold
Window panes

Or hillsides powder coated
Above the crest of suburban homes

We blew
Gas station

Air fresheners
Into

Glass pipes

And we sucked
Our souls' apparition

Rolling white clouds

Over a flame
Lapping at the bowl

As we turned it
Ten to two

And we drove
Ourselves

Into addiction

Without ever noticing

Your crazy neighbors

Who came out at night

Who Knew

Who knew

The greatest distance
Traveled

In one's life

Is out of the head
And into the heart

Call it
Emotional Bandwidth

The distance of a drink to mouth

Or

The distance
Of a homeless person

From your heart
To your wallet

As you walk

Or drive

By

Failing to notice

Blending in

Like garbage on the street

Death of a Dream

The ugly American's
Corporate body is bled

Lay off
By lay off

Death of a thousand paper cuts

Until
The American Dream

Is no
Longer on loan

The governments gone

Half way house
After Celebrity Rehab

Aligned in reruns of
Hollywood Stars

To place soul's
Foreclosure

On high resolution
Public displays

Of picture house
Perfection

We call it entertainment

And idolize those
Who fake their feelings

So we can feel our own

Reinforcing
Stories of otherness

No longer biblical

Somehow

The body

Of
The Church

Competes

But can't keep up

Audiovisually

Audiovisually

Noise Makes Heard

Noise
Stretches beyond music

Has grown into discussions

Which expand
The second

As yet impressive

More than landscapes

Dominated by lovers
Still growing

Fueled by time

Running to make
These quirky ambitions

Scope the overlapping audience
From out their own ethos

Interesting and vital

How taste evolves
From the suffer sound

Pigeonholed
As joined notes

Allowing time a measure of success

Eventually
Celebrating things alternative

And for many
Something like

Ascendance

To die shrinking into space

The degenerative world
Of the last thing keeping

Shows
We are all

Still noise

In great wide exposure

Single Mother

I'm over half my mother's age

And remember her
When she was mine

Braces and a perm

Sundae dinners
And slow dances standing on her feet

Listening to the crackle
Of records

Play

The $10 bill
I took off the dresser

She ran down the street
Still wearing her robe

Screaming
To the ice cream man

To take back

The ice cream
I had bought

All the neighborhood kids

Happy Hour
Hors d'oeuvres

Pulling a second chair next to mine

So I could
Lie and sleep

Beneath the white table cloth
At fine diners out

Taking a candy bar
At the grocery store

Under produce display

Where boxes gathered around
Made tunnels for me to hide and eat

Or following behind
Punching her butt

Or ramming it with the shopping cart

Just to get a reaction

Or tossing
Things

In the cart
When she

Wasn't looking

So she may not notice

When
Checking out

So often
Only about

Getting
What I wanted

To Date a Poet

I spill
Forth as

Words
Instead of wine

Having left the electric feel
Of the ethereal

I dated crazy
Insanely

Ego
Became

A pride of white lions

Roaring
In the dusty dusk

Of a darkening
African jungle skyline

Setting on the holy

War within

The magic of my mania
Fueled the relationship

Until it couldn't
Anymore

And there was nothing left
Between us

No more words

War within

Each Moment

Death becomes
More imminent

Watch how I
Unpack my ego

Tear the tight rope
Walk with words

As wire cutters
Unravel my mind

A tapestry
Of reality

Back lit
By your brain

Perhaps

Daylight
Illuminating

The movement of dust

In shafts of light
At a slant

From the open windows
Across the living room of your mind

Ghost of Dreams Realized

Though your possession
Has been exorcised

I still think I see a child car seat
In my side mirror

Every time I drive away

I recall
How we found

A home together

In each other's arms
And bodies

Entangled

Completely wrapped up

In someone else
Who felt like me

But now

The clouds cry for me

Splatter against
My car windshield

As my mind tries
To enter my body

Looking for a way back out
And into the world

Beyond the disillusionment

Of your manipulation
And deceit

Though I understand
It's not about me

Which allows me to accept
It never really was

Though I always tried
To make it so

As I drove away

You moved away

We were
Adult children

Who played
House too soon

So I could rescue you
And your children

Becoming family

Was an unplanned dream
Realized

And losing your children
In my life

Helped prepare me
To lose my own

Life and Death

As a child

I thought death
Might be sleep

Without dreams

In college
On acid

Looking out
My 10th floor dorm window

At the concrete quad below

I thought impact
Would be to wake up

And that very moment

Someone who knew me
Happened to look up

At the huge tall building

Noticed me
Standing at my window

In the middle of the night
And shouted my name

Snapped me back to reality

Saved me from becoming
One of those stories

Of someone on acid
Thinking they could fly

Depressed

A finger on a key
Of my keyboard

Spits the same letter
Across the page incessantly

bbbbbbbbbbbbbbbbbbbbbbbbbbbbbbbbbbbbbbbbbbbbbbbb

Cursor no longer blinking

Just stuck in a world
No longer able to stimulate

Brilliant blossom
Imploding within

How a sun dies
Into becoming

A black whole

Light matter
Becomes
Dark matter

And what matters
When all we have left

Is that which we cannot yet see

Hear
Feel

Taste
Or smell

Invading our minds

From just behind
Everything

In the stillness
That surrounds

How everything is in motion

Yet appears

As this

Here
Now

Fight Club

I

I drive through my past
Neighborhoods no longer home

Mental health is on the corner
Of Parkmoor and Bascom

In a wheel chair
Slumped over

Against a light pole

One hand
On the cross walk button

And the other

Down his
Pants

II

The beast I feed
Only turns on me

You are merely the excuse

I use

To feed it

    III

I offer you escape

From the sun having set on your life
And no moon to remind you

Of your slow suicide
As you drink poison

To build a tolerance
For unwanted emotions

    IV

I want to ask you what the opposite of suicide is
Suggest

You don't fuck
With crazy

Even criminals know that
Especially locked up

Pleading insanity

Which is almost all
That keeps me safe

From myself
Reacting

To those
Who meant

To hurt me

But decided
Instead

To be friends

    V

I wore your snake skin
Too long

And slithered
In hot sweat

Shedding hate

The dead of me
You are

Romancing the Stoned

I drove off mountain highways
Into Purple Kush skylines

Setting on
Acid rainbows

Over champagne
Waterfalls

Funneled

Into college
Mentalities

We studied kegs
Red Solo cups

And Catholic school girls

On Mission lawns
Sunbathing

Textbooks
Wide open

Legs in the air
Playfully

While they watched us
Shirtless

Throwing Frisbees
Purposely

Their way

To make contact
Conversation

In hopes of conversion

Hitchhiking to Heaven

Recovering alcoholics
Say they don't miss the hangovers

I didn't mind drinking more
To get over mine

But

It's the emotional

Hangovers
I hate

Especially

Without a drink
Or drug

To alleviate the pain
Of my choices

At least
Today

I know the true cause
Of my problems

It's me

Even

Clean and Sober

I can be
Dry and reckless

As I struggle with my darkness

Learn to slow dance
With my shadow

Instead of letting it
Wrestle me

To the ground
From behind

Beat down
And dying

Where people
Found me

Passed out
Under a car

Bleeding to death

Blues Undone

I undressed
Attempted to wipe

You away

With my
Bare hands
And a bar of soap

The suds
I lathered

In warm water

Rose all around me
Releasing

The blood of your lamb
I no longer drink

Because decayed fruit
Is a decadent poison

I sought

To destroy my pain

Without realizing

It would cost
My life

Yet

I came to

Once again
Saved

Perhaps

So I could write
My way

Out of myself

And share it
With others

All the
Strangers

Who came to my rescue
Time and time again

This time
I come to my own rescue

So not to bleed out
But for these words

I write
Realizing

My own son
Sits in front of me

And a moment of
Alcoholic clarity

Comes to me
Sober

After all of these years

It is time to stop bleeding
And be with him

Fade Into You

I

We closed the door

To hide
From graffitied walls

And words I wrote
On the ceiling

Paint
Cracked

And homemade mobiles

Short straws and lines

Turning ever so slightly
In the breeze

From open windows
In old Victorians

II

I couldn't comfort
Your growing hysteria

Any more than wine
And marijuana

With steak
Cooked in butter

After a vegan
Diet

    III

We offered each other
Our light

As sacrifice

Until afraid
Of our shadows

Peering out
From behind bent blinds

As city people
Scurried about

Like cockroaches
In the light of day

IV

We worked on your
Still frames

In a dark room
Exposing

Our Negatives

V

My life became defined
By chasing

One peak moment
To another

My mind
At war

With my brain

VI

We abducted each other

Held hostage
In worm holes

As we wore stars out
Of our black hole brains

Allowing access
To what felt

Like transcendence

To burn in the moment
Completely

Until finally full of nothing

But the nightmares
Fishtailing

Our streams of consciousness

Spilled out before us
On the floor

Our minds
And hearts

Empty

Grief and Loss

People have been telling me
How strong I am

But the real strength
Is yet to come

So many
Have gathered

In love
To celebrate

My beautiful boy's
Life

All the prayers and hugs felt
From near and afar

Have sustained me
While I have been working through

The shock and awe of it all

As I hide

In the farthest corner
In my mind

As I wade
Through all

That is yet to come

As I try to live

Face the day

As others
Go back

To their lives
Leaving me

To find my way

As emotions
Come up

From the absolute depths
Within

And challenge my existence

I had to admit
I need the help

And find the courage
To ask for it

And the fortitude
To find it

And the willingness
To see it through

Because each day is different

And what it takes
To get through today

The best I can

May not work
Tomorrow

And

It is up to me
To learn

How to take
Care of myself

Through such grief
And love lost

But I cannot do it
Alone

Though often
It feels that way

Even around people
Who love me

So I pray

When the times come
When the pain is too great

I will surrender
My suffering

And share with others
Who can help me

Carry the load

From one moment
To the next

And do whatever it takes
To get through

Whatever

Comes my way

Too Many Stories

I let too many people in today
And got overwhelmed

Trying to listen
In light of my loss

As people talked at me
I heard only noise

And wondered
Why they were making it

But there is no story
Especially theirs

Right now

That can change
How I feel

Because I am
Out of my mind

Until I notice

The sun
Hot on my skin

The sound of children
Playing in the park across

El Camino Real

As the 22 line
Double bus

Pulls away
From Shoreline

A silver and black
Harley Davidson

Accelerates
Through an intersection

Rips a tear in my mind

Letting me
Spill

My reality

Into poetry

We All Lose People We Love

Grieving the loss of a loved one
Especially a child

Being bipolar
Addict
Alcoholic

And Codependent
With sleep Apnea

Has its challenges

Because
I struggle

To breathe
At night

Or
To help myself

Especially when
Drugs and alcohol

Seem to be a solution
To my pain

Even though
They make me want to die

So I feel the need
To take care of others

Before
Myself

Because I can't face
The mess I've made

And the work
I need to do
To clean it up

So I must do for myself
What no one

Can do
For me

And act as if

80

I know how

To care for myself
As I need to do

Until eventually

My self-care
Practice

Teaches me how

To actually
Really

Care about myself
For the first time

I can't do this on my own
Though it is up to me to do it

Whatever it is
Whatever comes

I must surrender
Accept

And be honest with myself
And others

About what is
Really going on

Inside of me

As each
And every day

Is different

Each sun that sets

Leaves a new darkness
We must

Fend and find
For ourselves

A way to live though

Feeling
Smaller and smaller

Until we are nothing

Because everything
Can become overwhelming

And all we can do
Sometimes

Is breathe

But even that

Can be
Hard to do

Especially

When anxiety
Takes hold

And panic
Seizes your lungs

As you feel
Your mind

Swimming for a way out

Thoughts thrashing

Frantically
About

Drowning

Rolling
Through each other

And you almost welcome it

As an alternative
Solution

To feeling your feelings

And facing
The facts of life
Love and loss

Facing the music
When it doesn't play the song
You want it to

Or reminds you of something
You do not want to remember

It all comes down to surrender
I must surrender
Each and every day

To the God
Of my own
Understanding

Because faith in action
Works miracles

And faith in the miracles
To come

Gives me the hope
And strength

To carry on

Finding whatever I can
To best help myself

Now

Later

Tomorrow

And beyond

All I have ever
Wished for

Was what I have
Always had

Whether I knew it
Or not

Whether I felt it
Or not

In all things

Eventually
Love

Later

Some Words on Love

I come to you
In infinite forms

So that you do not forget me
But remember

Who you really are
And why you are really here

I do these things
Out of love

I do not expect love
For what I do

But to do
What I do

Out of love

Love
Is to know

I already gave

Everything

To you

Hope
Is to know

You are loved
And I

Expect nothing
But

To give this love
And share it

With others

Which has been so freely given
Us

If we are completely
Honest with ourselves

For what else is there
To do

But be
In love

In what and who
We really are

Because you are never

Truly
Alone

As I am
Always

With you

In Love

Mother & Father

Mother Earth
Clay from your soil

Father of the Light
Breathed spirit into

Our energetic roots
Tap

The very molten
Core

Of your transformative
Powers

As I root down

You relieve me
Of myself

And the energy I carry

Passes from me
To you

And is gone

The Father of Light
Gives me something

To strive towards

The light
And warmth

Of Love

And much like a tree
We grow

Down and up
Energetically

Suspended

Between

Two of the same
Source

With Father

Above me

And Mother
Below me

Nothing
Can be

Greater

Or
Less

Than
I am

Where you
Meet in me

I am

Mother Earth
And Father of the Light

I Know Better Now

I hear music
I used
To listen
To

To feel
My feelings

What once felt cool

Now makes me hot
And mad

Because I struggled

And am not
The same

Person
Anymore

But I still
Struggle

With myself

And everything
I am

And am not

Wrestle
With
Myself

Like my
Step Father

After he had
Enough

To drink
Just before
He had

Too
Much

When I was

94

Too
Young

To understand

And believed
His words

Face to face

Like
Fire

Breathing
Dragons

I had

Nightmares
As a child

Alcoholic

Breath
Burning

My
Face

I was always
Their problem

He even told me so
After my Mom left

What once brought joy
Brings pain

Because
I grieve

Losing who I was
And not

Really
Having

Or knowing
Who I am

Anymore

Which is all

Up to me
Now

To find my way
Through my pain

And sorrow

To travel
The distance

This all
Sets me apart

From myself

More than
Ever before

Because
Who I was

Only survived
What he survived

And

I may need
More of myself

Than ever before

The facts and feelings
Of my life

My thoughts
My actions

I am
Responsible

For my
Experience

There is no one else
To blame

Now

And there never really was

The Brave New World

My body

Shifted
And shuttered

Like a train

On subway
Tracks

As your
Voice

Guided me

Into the heart
Of my body

And the basement
Of my soul

I built a sky scraper
Of my mind

So I could dwell

In the crown chakra
Penthouse

Of my head

And look down
Upon everything

For the greatest view
And distance

Where
My ego

Is king

But just below

In my throat
I choke on my grief

Pain
Comes in waves

100

Contractions

As I prepare to birth
Myself

Anew

Not knowing how

To let go

Yet

I Lost My Child

Not in the mall
Or grocery store

Not in the park
At a county fare

But in a ditch
On the side of the road

Ejected from a car
Traveling too fast

Around a corner
Flipping on its top

Sliding off the road
And up into a tree

Where my son's lifeless body
Was found by his friend

Who drove

Who held him in his arms

Begged for him to wake up

While he gurgled
His last breath

Before passing on

Into the arms

Of his

Recently deceased
Uncle

Waiting for him
Just on the other side

Where we may
Meet again

One day

Any day

Now

Acknowledgements

I want to acknowledge all the love and support I've received through the years from family, friends, acquaintances, and strangers. I couldn't have done it without you all! I especially appreciate the families who have taken me in over the years and loved me as their own, the Whites, Hagamans, Averys, and Basaneses. You all have helped me through some of my hardest and darkest times. You all believed in me when I didn't believe in myself. I am eternally grateful for each and every one of you, and all who have known me and been a part of my life. Everyone I know has helped me in one way or another, whether you realize it or not. Thank you!

I want to think Ed Basanese for his friendship, encouragement, and support. Ed pushed me to write when I most needed it. He also supported my writing by reading, revising and editing my work over the years.

I want to thank Erik and Palamedes Publishing, for seeing the importance of this project and supporting it. I want to think Kate Marchio Photography for some of the images and design of the cover. I also thank her for her encouragement and support.

Most of all I want to thank Monica Martin, for her images, support, and inspiration. She helped me start writing back when we met in photography class in

104

college. I started writing regularly after attending her Senior English major reading. She has been a great friend and life partner. I have learned and grown more with her than in any other time in my life. Monica also connected with my son, Gabriel, in a way he and I had never known. They were two peas in a pod. We were both blessed to have her in our lives and experience real family soul connections. Monica has been by my side, in one way or another, throughout my life, and recovery. I am eternally grateful for her, and her love and support. Her images are what make up the cover design, and document a session where we worked through some of my deeper emotions I had not yet been able to feel since the loss of my son.

Creativity, healing, and recovery all work together for me and for that I am grateful as well, for finding a way through the darkness within, and the light without.

About the Author

Tavius Dyer is native to Northern California. He grew up in the San Francisco Bay Area, then moved to the California Sierra Foothills to a small town where he finished high school. In college Dyer began writing after witnessing a poetry reading on campus his freshman year. Writing became a personal, creative passion and lifelong daily exercise through regular journaling.

He struggled with mental health, addiction, and grief from loss of his only child. He learned to write through his wounds and into his shadow to find the light. Writing was an invaluable tool in his recovery, self-awareness, and spirituality.

He believes giving light to our shadow is an important aspect of personal growth and one's spiritual journey. He shares some of his experiences in *Shadow Work*.

Recent Publications

- Ingrid Arulaid, StepMOMs' Infinite Love, the pain of divorce overcome by magical love
- Carlos Hiraldo, Machu Picchu Me, urban poems growing into mountains
- Erik Pihel, Manhattan, a mini-epic poem about New York City
- Gill Puckridge, Gillybean in China, adventures of a wandering sexagenarian

Classic Ebooks

- A Gathering Darkness: 13 Classic English Ghost Stories
- Tradition Digitized: Ancient Poems in Modern Streams
- Joseph Conrad, Heart of Darkness
- Stephen Crane, The Red Badge of Courage: An Episode of the American Civil War
- James Joyce, Dubliners
- D. H. Lawrence, The Border Line: Soldier Stories by D. H. Lawrence